CASTING
STONES

Also by the author

COMING CLOSE

CASTING STONES

Helen Chasin

LITTLE, BROWN AND COMPANY
BOSTON–TORONTO

First Edition
To6/75

Some of these poems have previously appeared in the following
periodicals: *Barn Dream Press, The Harvard Advocate, The Iowa
Review, Partisan Review, Poetry, Quetzal, The Radcliffe Quarterly.*

The poem "Noon" appeared originally in *The New Yorker.*

"Thinking About Paradise" first appeared in *The Logic of Poetry,*
edited by John Briggs and Richard Monaco, McGraw-Hill, Inc., 1974.

"Photograph at the Cloisters" first appeared in *No More Masks!* edited
by Florence Howe and Ellen Bass, Doubleday/Archer Books, 1973.

The author is deeply grateful to The Radcliffe Institute and to The
Howard Foundation for their assistance.

Library of Congress Cataloging in Publication Data

Chasin, Helen.
    Casting stones.

    Poems.
    I. Title.
PS3553.H34C3   811'.5'4   75-5550
ISBN 0-316-13822-3
ISBN 0-316-13823-1 pbk.

*Published simultaneously in Canada
by Little, Brown & Company (Canada) Limited*

Printed in the United States of America

To   Phil

CONTENTS

CASTING
STONES

NEWS

It took its time getting here.
Meanwhile we opened animals like books
and ate the information. Their bones
were weapons, tools. We carved
the skulls and adored them
using the skin and guts to do music
to do rain and bring the sun around, to grow.
We taught the little ones how.
The first law was: news. We waited
a lifetime, many
getting better at it. After that
the news came to us. And the second law.
We worked the skulls beautifully and went on.

FIRE

The air was pure anger. It lit
and coiled, swirling
gin into gin, clear poison snakes

they drank their tails
all the way, and died of it.

Breathing was worse than my Screaming Dream where
I try telling *it hurts* and they're glad for me
so grief boils in the bloodstream like rage.

After the smoke put the air out
it rested, hanging over a while: weather
from World War Two or what's coming

then the burnt light began sifting, the day
falling back down, grains of it, black
feathery stuff, skin, the next day
was dirt in the mouth, then all the time
a taste of scar tissue, a feel to the eyes of weeping
as if someone had tried to kill   kill or die.

FIRE SIGN

The fire liked us, going to
take us with it . . . such confidence
must know something. And if it wants to that much.
And maybe it means we're good, maybe
we're news: implements, the wheel, open-heart.
But not mine, not now.
The fire went down whispering   next time

everything says so, beginning with
how mornings break out wild yellow. And smoke
in the fall stillness like haze. The trees rusting
is another. When the day clears
its pale air is good for doing things in   let's
while we can   have a look at the leaves, the ashes
right here reads like *soon*

the way some are being tried
as usual, it works, a few ruined
a number do it themselves
some talk of living differently.
Right here looks like out there in America
these end-of-the-world sunsets, like last night's

rage at the movies, burning love on the jukebox
the after-hours bar with its light the color
of booze, the feeling of
this-is-it. Look here
in the whiskey glass, and the red
of the red wine: the past, the place
in flames, dense
as rain forest. Somewhere a whole country's gone up.
It feels like always, like ours, the smell of breathing.

PERSPECTIVE

From now on back, love

there never has been anyone else. The dead
have faces, said things
I think, maybe I read or made up, far off
and flat as an old tribal plate, rust-
colored.

You're *in* everything: weather, trees, the tree of life
in the carpet, the protein code, all you
wherever I look
like the northern people
who suppose the whole world from up there
and have more than twenty words for snow and none for time.

BEAST

Now I know
where I know you from: those times
when they had fantastic sex

on the way down from the mountain. And there's
the road that goes to the cave, or the day
out on the island everyone else went looking for
oh   apricots, figs   once
in the temple
the air pulled, there was
a shift of light . . .

he was an animal. You have his
shoulders, the same thickset neck, something vulgar
in all that muscling, the veins are maps of it
along your arms, heavy blue roadways, power lines
running your belly. Look how you stand squared off
and the way your body moves

closer like his, covers, moves in, the last-minute
hook to the side, head lowered
and heaving, pushing
the whole world, sweating, wet with it all over
and lifting, rising and
caught in the air a moment in the sounds he made
trying to talk to her
falling back into coming down.

ON THE VERGE

However many are with you, two
or a number there's the same murmury buzz
as trees in the country, a humming
like wires *she doesn't know who her friends are.*
Yes. A handful
of recognizable fools stand by, their hands out
like nets in the twisted air, not interesting

while you take on daylight. Remember
yesterday? how you kept at it, every breath
using some up . . . somehow you have to do it again

move the sun or close your eyes and outlast it.
And there's a way of slowing your heartbeat.
Are you asleep? listen
unless this continual drone is the new music
people are talking *what's to be done?* Wait

nights are better.
When the dark comes down it comes in, almost
information oh you are promised.
Meanwhile you turn clever

each word a quick brown fox jumping over.
Your eyes glitter: mirrors
are not as good at keeping the world out. And knives.
No you will hear nothing against the children.
You sit and smoke like a suicide.

ORIENTAL RUG

This is our tent, its carpet flowers
thick, the rich valley floor.
Some went off early
while it was cool, not far from dark
to look, to take care of.
Here love the light opens like leaves.
Morning tangles: the tree of life
putting out roots, vines, wineberries

a field of reds
full bloom: pieces of sun fall so
the sun is poppy-colored, the poppies flame.

THINKING ABOUT PARADISE

Imagine
Gauguin up and going that way: *au 'voir*
and he's off into the South Seas
sunset, your best daydream's bastard's *bon voyage:*
bad, leaving
the wife, the little ones like that
and those nine-to-fiving five days a week
for a living, for weekends
and for what?
                    You imagine a sun
that ripens his days and brown women
under it whose hot blood
swells their breasts like melons, their lips
push out and pout for his love-bites, their
eyelids heavy, half-drawn over dark bedroom eyes
and the skirts like pieces of bedspread, batiks
that unwrap like a curl of kumquat easier than
crooking a finger *come here,* barefoot
to begin with those women
fall to him like fruit, ah sweet
and that's all, no making something of it after. And
they feed him too and give him
a place to live, their system of trade's that simple.
What is it to him when the mailboat fails or shows up?
There's a whole ocean out there, it ends

tropical blue at his island.
                        You imagine the man
living your wildest hope
of sin: heat, jungle gin, the lush
flowers, skin, a few words, painting only when he wants

that land of delight you have him in: it's pure Gauguin
and the sea a clear, deep
sky blue there's no other use for
for him, he'll never ever sail out over it again.

THE HIGH PRIESTESS (TAROT)

Whose qualities crest and give in
to its pull is the sea-stone's, the moon's
crowned woman on her salt throne who
is done to, is filled
flourishing
like the rich odor of low tide: starfish, fruits
of the ocean, its night-blooming
dominions.
                    Their lady prevails
and obeys.
Palms and pomegranates climb her tapestry,
watersilk folds of her robe spill
into water, she holds the Law in her lap.

12

ARTAUD-

the-Coocoo, stuttering, tortures language back
that tears his mouth: bloodstained, rusty
crud in the little cuts in the corners, crumbs
of opium, he eats it
to brown-out
the skullsplitting
suns boiling like mad eyes in his mind's eye:
pain flakes on his lips, bitter
chocolate spit, coffee
shit, he loves his disease, it's his life.
Speaking clots what he's trying to say

"I want to give them the plague itself
so they will be terrified, and awaken"

so at his lecture — oh, everyone's there —
he does dying for them. His whole body's
a spasm, freezing: he sweats poison
until its wet heat thaws his fingers . . . his throat
tangles, trying to scream
fire! there's fire
in the gut, greasy rot, trying to swallow.
He burns with fever
and the burning that cures.
Its odor is everywhere, this agony

"mine, yes, and everyone who's alive"

le tout Paris runs from.
He's a piece of rigor mortis, *merde,* it's spreading . . .
pits, piles, the streets are clogging up, smoke
curdles the air, caca black.

In the dark he makes
lovetalk, words like that come as easy
as eating. "Between us there could be a murder."

BREAKING AND ENTERING

He came as if everything was right in its place
and I had called *come see*

how I live: no money, a few pieces
I like, some books I keep
to go back to

and see the way the sun moves
the reds of the carpet west, deep
and slow as the day goes
through the vines, the tree of life, and goes down.

Didn't you like the pictures? the feeling, didn't you
want to stay? and smoke. Have music, wine
the dark half of the world all night, easy
as daylight, waking up and still here
in the late afternoon, so now we have a whole day.
One more and we can say *remember?* and
we can say *I thought* . . . and then maybe saying *tomorrow* . . .

What didn't you like
of mine? the footsteps, the voice
too soon for you
who's there? who is that?
or too many questions, a chain: why, when, how
did it go wrong? isn't there something . . . there's nothing
to talk over. Oh

look here's the blue scarab ring out and
the topaz and how the air is all bruised.

TATTOOED WOMAN

Hurt? the needle's a nail, a pushpin
to fix the multicolors under my skin
as if I clot in pictures, the blood
royal blue, green, gold as well
as the usual in me and pain
makes a painting

a school of painting: *it's all material.*
                                    There's a snake
for a wedding ring and a scarab for luck
or a scorpion, the Middle Eastern way of saying it's all over
without words. Isn't this ankle chain as last-century
as a love-rash?
                        Near where the heart is
is my valentine, a garland, MOTHER with torn flourishes, tear-
drops. Those little satiny pulls are because of the children.
Numbers somewhere
I can't remember . . . maybe I heard about, or dreamed . . .
faded as birth stains by now.
And there's a skull here, its eyeholes
stare at the middle distance like God or a crazy person.
It has the depressive grin of a clairvoyant.
                                    See my

thighs all art nouveau
funeral flowers, blooming
                        and that
Chinese dragon a bruise, his tongue

16

is a burn, his scales
really grow there. Look how useful
the veins are where they show, a map, how long it took.
Someone laid tracks down on the wrists, then someone
x'd over, the old-fashioned look to it of patchwork, a piece
of advice: like this beauty mark, an asterisk, a star
from a touch of cancer.

ABORTION

Pulsar, bloodshot web, it

sucks down
clockwise. *Used water*
the drain chuckles. A red thread
unwinding to
all gone. Gotten. *All
out*. Clean:
that place where the stain was

clean as stone.

LEARNING
(For A)

Where are your eyes? and your mouth? your
smile? you
and a world out there to try
to take in, to cry for
the first half year with no color, no tears.

His eyes are very blue. Hers are
hard to tell: purple or green or brown
as the day goes, we'll see. Say bye-bye.
What does daddy do? What time is it? Simple as
A, down, tomorrow, one
and one more for grandma.

Was there snow then? the ocean? all over the world
sunlight falling or silver when it's going to rain
and good times to tell the children like stories.
Then what happened?

One day the children were walking
they had a language
they had scars, their own ways, mail
and looking back, and planning.

One day one of them said
I'll never forget right now

how the sun lights the Sunday morning
kitchen, sitting around after breakfast to talk.
The egg streaks on our white plates
are like those modern paintings we saw that time
bright yellow pieces of color, the shiny air
and feeling so good here, so clear
and when we're grown up telling the children.

D J C

He has it two hours before I know
a day's here, ours to do with
again, one of the seven: surprise.
Oh there never was an egg like this egg:
the yellow lake in the white cave
the giant swallows. Good.
He goes out to learn
what will give, because
this isn't fair, he gives it twenty years: the poor
people everywhere. *Why is the news always bad?*
The bus takes him to the Quakers teaching
schooldays. One day he made
something like sunset. Or sunrise. Or tangerines
and plums. *What's strange is interesting.* Blacks.
Women. His eyes shine like the time when.

MONA LISA, AGE 12

Her skin's not good, pale
and enraged at the same time.
Her whole sullen body's still baby
fat, no neck
to move swanlike
so she looks sly when she looks sideways
out of the family eyes, they always seem to know something.
Her mouth goes mean sometimes for no reason, her heart
breaks mid-sentence. Margins fill with her name.
She writes in her diary: sick
of them, of me, of nothing at all
happening, maybe I'll die
then they'll be sorry, too late
then the locked door, she takes
hours making herself up —
charcoal, colors, her own work
framed in the glass, practicing: come to me, kiss
off, guess, the girl in the story
about the girl taken by gypsies, or the one who's so good
she gives her life to God . . . whoever she is these days
is late again dear God all day the body clocks' slow going
to go through: tell her it will, it will be all right
and her mouth turns down the good word, she says
oh, yes?   with her eyes   interesting, almost.

NOON

Half-way
another day goes bad, impossible
to breathe or see by, the sky stone
gray, heavy, close
as the end of the world.
                              It feels like forever
to get through
until the tarnished air goes out, the light
is as dense and difficult
to move in as slow-motion.

Let's walk in the dark
and look at its true colors: the midnight
blue river and trees, the black
on black skyline, a sky must be up there

its moon a word in a dead language
about fire.

DISTANCE

All these problems are old ones: the rain

so many days of it now, of being
away from you and
of being away from your friends, the city you live in
the way its light falls, its rain.

Let's have it that there's a warp of one hour
between where you are and here

and suppose someone is *here,* almost half-way
using the year up like air, money
the work's going well, she knows a few people, a few
places to have a good time

say at midnight
they all go to the graveyard, see its black angel, and
some thought of music, and brought wine, so:
to the stones, darkness, the stars and everything
under them. And tomorrow. That smear in the sky line
that's the sun coming around, whatever happens
it isn't news. There were others.
There was moss. A mat of needles
to lie on, bedrock, salt flats.
And sand. There were seasons.
The worst of the ways of having a bad day
is this one. What if it happens again? take a breath
and again. Look at the gates. One more.
The marble babies. A pain like breathing. And
now? Oh! here's another, yes
the surprise of dying we have no right to
so many days of it.

AFTER THE BAD ENDING
(For E)

All this time his: so
the space of a room-
ful isn't anything, she hears

his eyelids, the pauses between saying
nothing and not saying a word
not lost on her over there:

bodies, objets d'art, smoke, music
are their molecules

no use, they loosen and slide
and make way, every moment
breaking in smaller pieces, they can't stop

his breathing, his nails growing, he's all new
every seven years, she hears it happen
each minute, he's beginning, half-minutes

just then, just now, now
his voice lays the air out in phrases

how it's been since, when was it, so many
changes, another person: still she's his
and he's her one real joy, pure, pure pain.

VAN GOGH'S LETTER

Writing a friend
about his river outing, how the boat
eases up the channel, the water unrolls and scenes
along the bank spread into scenery

for a while he's like everyone else
having a fine time: overhead
the sky is yellow.
After that the usual kind of close: the space
between them, until . . . meantime
his loneliness, his best, Vincent.

Then looking it over
look where he's gone back
to what's wrong, the lie within *is yellow*
because color means, it makes the afternoon.
He opens the sky and adds
grass leaf absinthe a feeling   he has to
to tell how everything really happened
he puts in ∧ *greenish-*

VINCENT DYING

"In my picture of the night café I have tried to show that the café is a place where one can ruin oneself, go mad, or commit a crime."

That part of his life Vincent lived
on coffee and nerves, whole days
of available light —
                    the palette opened —
landscape simmers in it
there's a skyful of warnings
the dark thickens into a crisis.

Nights went like the night before —
cheap wine, those cheap cigarettes
rotting the air like sweat
and bad feeling. And
the same feeling bad as always, brooding
over the poor, the meanest ah

it was poison, it made him crazy. Or
was he crazy to do it?
because of the stars, or his yellows   what a spin

the late summer
planets throbbing like lamps

in the fevery glare   what time is it?   in the ennui
the night café offers as atmosphere. Like here
in the picture, the place

is slow, no one uses the billiard table, no one's buying.
The owner has nothing to do
but look at the walls
and wait, something can happen. The walls
are blood red. Maybe it's afternoon outside

burning ochres and blues burning green. The air
is too brilliant, there's something final in it:
a wellbeing like the beginnings of grand mal
or something Vincent was trying to show he understood
when he shot himself *for everyone's good,* refusing
with twenty-four hours of leftover breath
to come back
to a sadness he said would otherwise last forever.

FOUND POEM

Dear Helen,
there is something I would likr to tell y u.
.there is something I would like totell you.
There is something I would like to tell you.

There is something I would like tootell you.

There is something I would like to tell yiu.

There is something I would like to tell you.

However there is something else I would like to tell you before.

MICK JAGGER AT MADISON SQUARE GARDEN

All of a sudden down there
they're streaming like protoplasm
so eager to go
telling time like lives to work out

only wait

something for all forty thousand of us
or more

he comes on at midnight.
All right. What a piece
of come-on, so tough
what a mouth, you get it all right.

Moving takes him, he's here, he's
here, he's
no one's bad boy, he's trouble

in his fag leotard, red scarf, flashing
stud belt Mick makes
wicked music, down there
they're dancing to it. In the balcony
men and their women are with him, trying
some light up and suck, the crazy air
hisses. He might for kicks take you, also
what you like, don't ask him to love it
or not laugh, he's AC/DC
as to God and politics, even sex
is easier than this
extreme case: he isn't nice
or not nice or not funny:
no satisfaction, satisfaction —
more than you want to know and live happy.

NO. 271: STANDING MALE FIGURE

in stone, Mexican

of a man when a man is an animal. He
stands back like a human being
surprised: his head is a coyote's
whose mouth is wide open. The tongue hangs down
damaged. See his genitals
are broken, frightening, and all those teeth
as he barks   *look out*   or howls
clamping his stomach as if that's where the hurt
comes from and he's about to
do something   he may   vomit   or kill.

MARRIAGE
(To C and J)

This man and this woman promised to live
sick, no money, or worse
the rest of their lives

now look.
A sentence sticks in his skin
like a fishhook; ripping fixes it
and hurts; these drops of serum
read like a trail. One of his looks
punches the oxygen out of her air, her heart
folds like the atom bomb run backwards.
That was close but both are still breathing.

What do we do now?
This wine is off. The candlelight
buzzes and winks, a little petit mal
and the turntable scrambles music
so it all comes out *work at making it work*.
What did you think?
Nothing. But not this.
These pictures of ten years ago look crazy

the white wedding
papers to sign
a house, children, party politics they agreed to
like names, lines for a death notice.

Bury this time package, listen, the carbon-14
runs down like a bad heart

so this man and this woman
can wake up making love learning each other
one more day, choosing, fighting
to live together
as long as they have left, their lives, maybe.

DECEMBER: NEW YORK

For some time now days have been
minimal:

gray up to noon, half way, the horizon

and over it a strip of air
like office light like eyestrain
no color at all but too much glare

then a blue stripe, the blue hour
as if we were happy, easy
to fall in love in

then a ribbon of violet
it's the edge of the world out there
pale as dawn, pale as dying

and a black band.

FLASHER

Zip! like that
he's past all the fuss, fumbling
around, propaganda. And so what if he's
dumber than if, o'clock, wanna? my place or
where? So no lousy promises, he says
what's what in body talk now
the sign of the goods
like the big shoe for the shoestore:
this here.

PHONER

My voices are there when I call, listen
and grow physical for me, opening
with *hello* or *yes* . . . that sort-of question
lets me in, then
I'm theirs.
When they agree to their names
I have them, make them
particular, every one has something I love:
shell pink ears, rosebud mouths. Scars
from what they've been up to. And a few
details that couldn't be someone else, I'd know
them anywhere. I tell them
what's good. I say how
I want them and how saying it
it happens, even the breathing's not nothing.
We're mouth to ear, ear to mouth.
I come into their lives talking, talking.

BOYS ARE

eager to do things
for her: read more, money and lovemaking
they never thought of until now.
And hard liquor, whole days going down
like health food, really fucked, a kind of cure.
Even leave her alone when she feels like.

I never did this before
but I could get into it. Is this *making a life?*
I'd be good for you

and so on. See that stuff piling up
all over the yard? offers
she filed in it and other trash, what a dump . . .

almost a garden there, lady, it needs
an afternoon, I will, and some red: let's have
a bed of poppies and happily-ever-after.

Oh what an angel face, isn't he
straight out of that old Italian picture? the one
with all the suffering where it's so beautiful
and all the trying to save.
The mouth-to-mouth could look like kissing —
a certain light, a distance
a minute it might work
the way they say love works . . . only
later, look where the sun's coming from:
you know what today is the first day of.

FUNERAL
(For RR)

Every day now the day goes out earlier: during
dinner, before-dinner drinks, rush hour, late afternoon
sometimes the day before

it comes down like fallout, falls
like dirt, the air's all used up. And the dead
are bodies in boxes, earth fills the holes in

no room to turn over, get up
what a bad dream, the dark made breathing too hard

but now we're here
let's walk in the grass. And let's have a good talk
we'll say what we're always leaving for next time now.

See the children running among the flowers, the stones
the children having a time, no shoes
like a place in the country, no idea of the time
all afternoon, they play until they can't see the game.

Doesn't this look like Stonehenge, the small markers
and sentinels, the sunstone?
Oh we forgot candles, and evergreen
and this side of the year
how quickly the bad light closes in.

JUST BEFORE SOMETHING HAPPENED

Five years and they're still speaking

whole days together, it looks more like lovers
that desperate *who are you?*   tete-a-tete
at parties, while the late movie's on and later
in bed, all morning   *not in front of the child*

as if there isn't enough time
in this lifetime for them
to say how
it's not working. They have a river view, monies
growing like grass, really good art
the other usual goods and
she wants out
of this happily ever after, the air in it
clotted as jailhouse air, the light sickroom light
and her hours wrap like that white cloth they use.

Oh but she promised, he needs her
to cook, to spin. *Let's play house. You be
and I'll be*

look, their light's still on: another
all-nighter, a morning he's not alone in
she needs being alone in to live. So

the sun comes up, an old problem, I and not-I:
say I is a person, she's calling for paper, pencils
and close the door like one of those crazy ladies.

What could she be doing in there?

DISSOLUTE

in Russian: Rasputin

said of being saved
you can't get to it from here, sin
is the place to start to be sorry
to be depraved.
And he meant it, went himself all the way
to Petersburg, and rerouted millions.

                                     What if
the worn-out blood, the overwrought
veins and royal family breaking again were
God's word to Nicholas? and his boy filled with it
like a disease: bruises, tearing, the tide
rising, red spilled out of its passageways
into streets, rivers
of it, the bandages
armbands, banners

and that one a tourniquet. Who knows how? The eyes
of course, and touching: some of those he laid hands on
felt flowing soul stuff and great peace after, some
he mumbled prayers to, or filth, some who didn't
go under easily he slammed.
Where he came from you met God
trying and failing, coming and falling
down drunk, in the dark
it snows all night, their winters almost all night.
The monk who stank like a goat could as soon screw
again as breathe, every inch

a move toward heaven.
                    His last evening
ten men's worth
of poison went like vodka. Shooting slowed him
enough for his assassins
to try murder: disposed of
in a pond whose ice closed over
as he maneuvered out of his handcuffs he drowned.

JUNE

This morning

except for the sunlight, its yellows
as deep as full summer
and these all-out greens

love it looks bad. And it feels
like from now on . . . remember when
we were so happy sometimes we wanted
to change our lives
almost enough to change our lives

what were we going to do? when
was it the universe turned on love, all
the important stories? Remember

those two, lying so close
in the Japanese suicide poster, they
could be making love, they might be sleeping
nude, thin-skinned as children: a tangle
of fine black lines, like briars,
a catch of barbed wire where the blood
red chrysanthemum grows, that's their wound
bright as the seal on a death-paper, a sun-
burst, a full moon pulling in
after a night of wild tides and dying.

THE POETESS KO OGIMI

her mouth an O
as if she's on to something
surprising
                or difficult, or doing
the lady's complaint or first-naming
her grief

leans, an apostrophe.
Her thin carpets heap and scatter
like pieces of paper, they sail like a raft, oh
she rides them, a survivor, looks out over
the beige sea slant-eyed.
                                Where
have the thirty-five others gotten to
or been left at?   Wherever

now she's alone. Her kimono sleeve
gestures at her breast.
Maybe there's a marriage, children, but not

here, just her
scarves flying, skimming
the air's strata, and
the rugs snaking like ribbons of low water
and no

pen or worksheets: pure process. Oh oh
she squats like any woman in some anguish
on those various colorful stuffs
crooning out of her Japanese hair.
Will she never leave off? Unless
here is the hereafter
death will get her to.

Painting attributed to Fujiwara Nobuzane. The Poetess Ko Ogimi: for-
merly part of The Scrolls of the Thirty-six Poets, 13th century.

SELL

His is a service, like ice: the old
odd hours, late
aren't you going to ask me in? the smile
a wound, the usual news about God
in his eyes, deep
silver: maybe there's hope. He tells you
you and other interesting stories

there's gold in that voice, a music
not so easy as love but like it
the way to do your life from now on:
the pain is a good sign
there's no saying no, look at the dead.

PHOTOGRAPH AT THE CLOISTERS
(For C and H)

This is where we're at the gate.
What a time we had getting here:
the sun's at half past, see the lines
in our faces, and our hands
are maps: what happened
and how we could go if we wanted.

Think of being happy this way: long walks
and stone quiet, the colors
pure light, a cell
of your own   *prière ne pas déranger*
oh I know that voice.
And not having to pull the sun up, to plan
the evening.

Whenever it was when you were a girl
when you thought about being a nun
were you lovely? in black
in pain always more beautiful
than a dead lady, waiting.

Look at us, how long our hair is.
Imagine: you've just given your husband up
and those children over there have my smile
they're waving, *ciao,* my way
of saying goodbye. Think of a woman
burning the way days do.
The flowers are fireworks, they flare in their spaces
like stars for words for doing something terrible.

DOING THE I CHING
(For J)

The three of us are throwing pennies
to find out about love and work, how we can live
away from
if we have to, how long

and how can we live where we are? more
than not dying, deeper than the breathing they give you
to get you through, the talk   *well you have yourself*   ah

we have the three of us
doing our slow Sunday afternoon in October
drinking doing the Book of Changes. The trees
and the coins are the same color, the five o'clock
fall mist almost rain. What is the situation
with Mrs. K, writing, the midwest: we get thunder, a time
of year, there's fire
in the lake, and coming back
but not now. *I should have known, I knew it.*
What about X? And the children.
We're doing the I Ching like telephone calls.

It is so vacant here, so flat I have done nothing
since yesterday but think about

time zones between us. And some leftovers
from different lives
we still have to deal with   *suppose I ruin this?*
like an only child, the other woman.

                              Maybe we're all alone

because we do it so well because we want to: a relief
like the laws of falling, their music
the small coppery drop of early stones:
pieces of bone that make numbers that make pictures
we're trying to read, look
we're in them. There's rain, darkness, and there *you* are
next year, or whoever that is, love
he's marvelous. I am afraid of what I'll do.